Look for These Upcoming Issues

Jon & Jayne's Guide to Throwing, Going to, and "Surviving" Parties

Jon & Jayne's Guide to Getting Through School (Mostly Intact)

Jon & Jayne's Guide to Teen "Flings" ('n Other Guy/Girl Things)

Issue #1 is dedicated to
Kaitlyn, Skylar, Eric, & Friends.

Thanx for everything!

Jon & Jayne

Jon & Jayne's Guide to

Making Friends & "Getting" the Guy (or Girl)

HCI TEENS™

Health Communications, Inc.
Deerfield Beach, Florida
www.hcibooks.com

AVERAGE BUT XTRAORDINARY

The authors believe the information and advice presented in this book are sound and relevant. However, it is recommended that you seek the help of a certified professional if you are facing serious challenges in your life. This book is not intended as a substitute for consulting with a professional mental-healthcare practitioner.

The term "hookup" as used in this book refers to hanging out with someone you like and making your feelings known.

The pseudonym "Jon and Jayne Doe" represents a creative and qualified collective of teens and adults. All characters in this book are fictitious unless listed as one of the crew (see pages 113–117).

The Library of Congress Cataloging in Publication Data is available through the Library of Congress.

ISBN-13: 978-0-7573-0659-4 • ISBN-10: 0-7573-0659-4

Printed in the United States of America.

Publisher: Health Communications, Inc.
3201 S.W. 15th Street
Deerfield Beach, FL 33442–8190

Illustrations on pages 73 and 106 by Judith Hans-Price.

"Dr. Toni" caricature by Larissa Hise Henoch

Cover design and interior design by Carol and Gary Rosenberg

PASSWORD: |

This book is your password to getting
to know yourself and the people
around you a little bit better.

It's the key to something new & fun,
a different way to view the world.

If you forget your password,
the hint is . . . *Jon & Jayne*.

Live

WHAT'S INSIDE . . .

WOW* 1

Chat **5**

The Scenarios 7

Oh, the Drama! 11

First Impressions **13**

Imagine 27

My Foot Said What?! **31**

Let's Get Conversing! 35

Courage, Confidence, and Charisma 41

Clique Here 53

Acquiring Acquaintances **67**

The LOVE Broker 69

He Said, She Said 73

You've GOTTA Hear This! 75

Conundrums & Solutions 85

Vent 95

Quickie 104

Got Satisfaction? 107

Tell the World 109

CYA! 111

Meet the #1 Crew 113

Where Can I Find? 118

FEATURING STORIES BY:

- Ashley K.
- Betania C.
- Billy M.
- Crystal G.
- Eric D.
- Franklin B.
- Joseph C.
- Kait R.
- Lexi S.
- Samantha D.
- Shari R.
- Taylor W.

WOW*

Hey, we're Jon Doe & Jayne Doe (no relation, just good friends). We represent people like you who want their voices heard **LOUD & CLEAR.**

Our world is the world of 7Fs*: friends, fun, fights, family, feelings, fashion, and flirting. It's a lot like your world! We have concerns about the future (another "F"!) and about getting by in school (no "F" for that) and in social situations. It's not always easy, and sometimes it's really hard. But we all seem to get thru it somehow.

We want you to be part of our circle of friends. We want to know what you—and people like you—have to say. Sharing our feelings on different subjects can help us to make sense out of this 7F world.

---

* **W**elcome to **O**ur **W**orld

*See my 7F protest on page 2. —Jon

Things like how to make friends, how to get that guy or girl to notice you, and how to be true to yourself seem so basic, but these are important issues that we deal w/ every day. They are so basic that we might not even consciously think about them.

Here, in this book, we do think about them, talk about them, complain about them, shout about them, and whisper about them. Why not, we've got a lot to say . . . and we bet you do too!

Be Heard. Be Yourself.

MY PROTEST

I told Jayne this whole 7F thing is
bogus. She thinks it's cute & catchy.
WHATEVER, Jayne, you know it's in
this issue under protest! -Jon

Duly noted and ignored.
—Jayne

You owe me. —Jon

Hmm, we'll see about that ;)
—Jayne

JONANDJAYNE.COM

Log on to our website,
www.jonandjayne.com,
and join the 7F community.
Post conundrums, share stories,
tell the world, take the surveys,
get answers to the quickies,
solve the drama,
and more.

See u there
& in here!

LiFe

cHaT_

JaynE SaYs 611: jon r u there?

JD GaTEr 110: yeah jayne whatsup

JaynE SaYs 611: did u c the new girl in bio?

JD GaTEr 110: how could i miss her? she's fine.

JaynE SaYs 611: hmmm.... did u talk 2 her?

JD GaTEr 110: nah did u?

JaynE SaYs 611: no but i felt bad 4 her

JD GaTEr 110: y

JaynE SaYs 611: starting right in the middle of the year not knowing anyone

JD GaTEr 110: i guess thats tough

JaynE SaYs 611: i'll talk 2 her 2moro

JD GaTEr 110: good tell her andys got a crush on her

JaynE SaYs 611: already???

JD GaTEr 110: like i said shes fine.

JaynE SaYs 611: hmmm. maybe its u thats crushin

JD GaTEr 110: hmmm maybe not. i like someone else

JaynE SaYs 611: oh like who?

JD GaTEr 110: i'll never tell

JaynE SaYs 611: jon!

JD GaTEr 110: night jayne

JaynE SaYs 611: wait

JD GaTEr 110: c u 2 moro

JD GaTEr 110 has signed off.

JaynE SaYs 611 has signed off.

What's your story?

THE SCENARIOS

Where do you fit in?

- **In a new space?** Maybe you just moved or started a new school, or a new grade, and you're a little rusty at making friends. Moving away from everything that's familiar can feel very scary. New faces, new sights and sounds, being the stranger in a crowd—so much is happening around you and you want to be part of it. You're just not sure how to go about it.

- **Got friends. Need girl?** Hanging out with the guys every Saturday nite doesn't seem to be cutting it for you anymore. You want some company of the female type, but you get tongue-tied or caught up in trying to act cool and distant when you're around girls. It's not getting you anywhere, is it?

- **Crushing on a guy?** Got your eye on that one, don't you? You're wondering how to get his attention, how you can get to know him, and how to be true to who you are at the same time. You've got Qs on your mind and want some As to those Qs.

- **Quiet, maybe shy?** You might feel like you never know what to say or how to say something that's on your mind. When you're feeling like this, it can be hard to imagine yourself opening up and making friends. But we all need friends to some degree, so we'll try to help you make that first step. It may seem scary, but all you need is a little courage.

- **Stuck in a clique?** Maybe you feel it's time to expand your horizons and step outside your social circle—your comfort zone. You're probably looking forward to approaching new people and situations w/ an open mind.

- **Something to say?** Maybe you've got a lot to say, and it sometimes seems like no one's listening. In this issue you'll find an outlet for sharing your words and views . . . we're listening!

- **Just curious?** OK, so you just want to read a good book and get to know what we're all about. You wanna know what people like you are thinking on matters that concern us—some are important, some are trivial, but they all matter one way or another.

Move on

In this **issue**, you'll find 5 keywords. You'll need these to unlock the **clues** to the **Drama**.

How will you know when you find a keyword? **Easy.** We'll say something like, "So, the keyword here is ________." Couldn't make it much easier than that!

When you find a keyword, go to jonandjayne.com, click on "Oh, the Drama" and follow the instructions. Each keyword unlocks a clue. Solve the drama in as few clues as possible.

GOOD LUCK!

ACKKK!
NO INTERNET?!
SEE PAGE 110.

Oh, the Drama!

Hey, Jon here . . .

Jayne's acting all "hurt" cause I don't remember her favorite song. Really, don't I have better things to remember—like the name of the new girl in bio?! (jk, Jayne.)

Can you help me figure it out?

OMG! I've only mentioned this song to Jon like a bzillion times!

The keyword here, Jon, is "LISTEN."

—Jayne

Honesty

FIRST IMPRESSIONS

No matter which scenario you identify with, you usually need to start with first things first: **first impressions.** Whether you want to make friends or meet someone you like, **think** about the impression **you** make on people.

Our first rule of first impressions is **be yourself**, BUT but be your BEST self. Think about the words you use to describe yourself. Put them in two columns: **positive** and **negative.** Then focus on showing the positive ones when you meet new people. We can't hide the negative parts of our **personalities** all the time, but we can let people get to know our **good** side first.

Positive	Negative

We all have our **quirks**, and there's nothing wrong with that—you just might not want to exaggerate your **quirkiness** for the sake of getting noticed. Exaggerating any part of your **personality** is a good way to make a negative first impression.

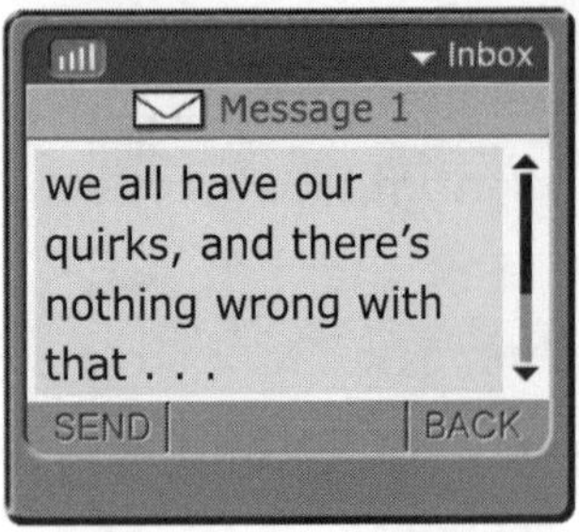

With less desirable traits like always being pessimistic or **sarcastic**, you might want to tone them down a bit. It seems like some people just can't help being this way, but it might give **others** the

impression that they're not interested in making new friends and would rather be **alone**. This probably isn't true. Keep in mind that people are less likely to **approach** you if you've always got a **frown** on your face.

Think about how you look, too. You don't have to be a **cheerleader** or a jock to look good and make a good impression. **Work** with what you have to make **yourself** presentable and approachable. It's a good idea to **avoid** doing things to your appearance that you don't feel **comfortable** with, but don't be **afraid** to try new outfits or hairstyles.

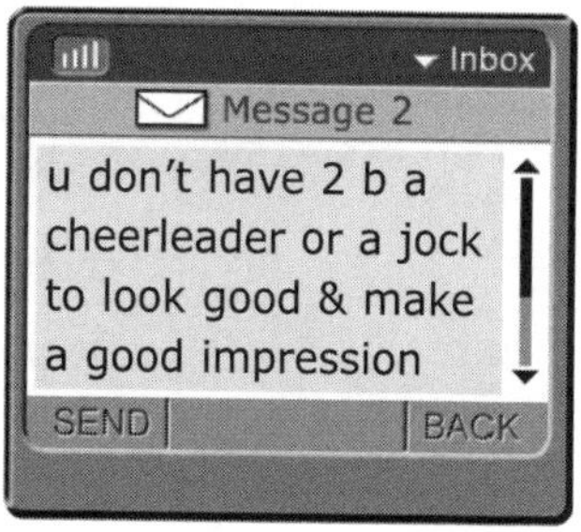
Inbox
Message 2
u don't have 2 b a cheerleader or a jock to look good & make a good impression
SEND
BACK

Keep your head up, your eyes and **mind** open, and be **approachable**. Think about your body language. If your head and eyes are down and you don't make eye **contact**, you're likely sending a **signal** to others that you are unapproachable—whether you mean to or not. There's more on this in "My Foot Said What?!" on page 31. Check it out!

Lexi's Story

Judging a Book by Its Cover

One of the hardest things about being a teenager is making new friends. I usually look for certain things in a person before walking over to say hi. That's not the way it should be, but it's hard not to pay attention to first impressions. For me, I look at what the person is wearing, their hygiene, and the way they look at me.

For starters, if a girl is wearing all black, chances are she just isn't my kind of person. I'm not saying this is true for all people, but to me, all black means they are rough and hard, not so easygoing. On the other hand, if a girl is wearing all pink, I probably wouldn't go up to her either. To me, all pink means she's spoiled and probably thinks she is all that. Don't get me wrong, that's not always the case, but in my life usually it is. I'm more likely to say "Hi, what's up?" to a person wearing regular clothes—nothing too extreme—because that means to me that she's not trying too hard to get noticed.

Hygiene is the second thing I look at. I most likely would not approach someone who looks like they haven't showered in days, or if their hair is all ratty looking. It makes me think they don't care if they have friends or not. The way a person presents herself in this way is really important to me.

Another thing I notice is the way a person looks at me. That also plays a big part before I walk over to someone. It helps more if it is an inviting look, or maybe just a smile. A look that says, "I'm better than you," "I'm not interested in you," or "You need a makeover" is all I need to turn the other way. I mean, why would anyone want to hang out with someone like that?

It's hard not to judge a book by its cover. I do it even though I know it's not the best way to be. Unfortunately, people are going to be judged. No one is perfect—not the people who are doing the judging and not the people who are being judged. I wish I wouldn't have to go by first impressions before I go over to make a new friend, but that's how it is going to be, at least for now.

Lexi S.

We love Lexi's honesty. Lots of people might say they give everyone a chance no matter what. But we know that's not always true.

All black, all pink, that's a matter of personal taste, of course. If you feel comfortable in the colors you wear, don't let Lexi's opinion of what they represent change your mind. It's good to be aware, though, that some people will have preconceived notions of who you are by what you wear. All that's important is that you be yourself when choosing your clothes and colors. We say anything goes!

Lexi's right about personal hygiene. Not showering is a good way to turn people off! And how someone looks at you or how you look at someone that very first time you make eye contact may play a major role in whether or not you become friends. It pretty much all starts there.

Shari's Story

Clumsy Me

When I was in 8th grade, I was crushing on this boy Joshua, but he had no idea I was even alive. He was sooo cute, and I'd think about him all the time—I couldn't get him or his brown eyes out of my mind. He was a grade ahead, so we weren't in any classes together. We didn't even have the same lunch period. I didn't know much about him other than he had lots of friends and was part of the cool crowd. I wanted him to notice me so badly.

Once I figured out when our paths would cross between classes, I made a plan. You wanna know what my brilliant idea was? I decided that when I saw Joshua, I'd drop my books, he'd help me pick them up, and the rest would be history. So when the time came between third and fourth period, I put my "goof-proof" plan into action. There he was and there were all of my books flying thru the air. They just exploded out of my arms, papers going everywhere. "Oh, no!" I shouted.

Joshua looked at me, right at me! It worked, my plan worked! He was going to stoop down and help me just the way I had imagined. I gave him a little smile, pretending to be embarrassed, and bent down, never taking my eyes off of him for a second.

He didn't reach down to help—just looked at me for a second, then smirked.

"Clutz," he said, as he stepped around my books and walked away.

Shari R.

LOL! Sorry, Shari, but you have to admit, that scheme wasn't very goof-proof.

Sometimes we do crazy things to get attention. When we create elaborate schemes to get what we want, they have a tendency to backfire. Shari probably would have been better off just saying hi to Joshua whenever she saw him in the hallway. Even a smile might have helped to break the ice.

Anyway, a guy who is really interested in a girl probably wouldn't go out of his way to make her feel foolish—even if she did a foolish thing. Nobody likes being called a clutz—even if it's true.

Joshua gets ☹ ☹ ☹ ☹ from us.

Billy's Story

The "Weird" Kid in Art Class

It was my first day of art class one summer. Sitting next to me was some weird-looking kid who loved music and art. Most of the kids were talking behind his back, saying things like, "What's up with that kid?" or "What a freak." But he didn't seem to notice at all. I admit, I thought, *What a weirdo,* to myself too, but something inside me also told me to talk to him.

At first I didn't know what to say, but I finally found a few things to talk about. We ended up in a whole conversation about the things we liked to do. Each class, we talked more and more, and I found out that he was into the same kind of music as me. We also had a similar art style and had some of the same hobbies, like skating and playing guitar. I started to look forward to art class just to talk to him some more.

We ended up hanging out together almost every day that summer. We drew, listened to music, played guitar, rode our bikes, and went to skate parks.

But once school started, we didn't talk so much and sort of just stopped being friends. We went to different schools, so it wasn't like we'd see each other there. A few months into the school year, we had to do a paper on what we did that summer. That's when I remembered the "weird" kid in art class and how cool it was hanging out with him.

So I called him up and we started hanging out after school and on the weekends. We introduced each other to our other friends, but they didn't really get along. So, most of the time it was just the two of us.

That was two years ago, and we're still great friends. I could've just said he's too weird for me and never made the first move. It turns out he's not weird; he's unique, and so am I, and we like it that way. I think it's amazing that just a few words that Saturday morning turned into a great friendship.

Billy M.

If Billy had gone by first impressions, he and that "weird kid" in art class would never have become friends. And what's "weird" all about anyway? Just because someone looks or acts different from the crowd doesn't make them weird.

Sometimes we need to give people a chance to show us their personalities to decide if we want to be friends with them. Maybe we'll find out we don't like that person, but maybe we'll find out that we like the same things. We'll never know if we don't take that first step and say, "Hey."

Jayne's advice on

HOW to IMPRESS a GUY

- Be yourself! Be confident!
- Show interest in his hobby or sport (if it's sincere).
- Ask Qs about things that matter to him.
- Look your absolute best (but don't go overboard).
- Smile a lot and flirt a bit.

Jon's advice on

HOW to IMPRESS a GIRL

- Listen (really) to what she has to say.
- Be cool. (Whatever that means to you.)
- Look good and maybe brag just a little.
- Answer her MANY questions honestly.
- Smile or laugh when she says something cute or funny.

Imagination

Imagine.

Imagine.

What did you imagine?

It could have been **anything**—or maybe it was **nothing**. Maybe you just flipped the page or maybe you stopped for a minute and **thought** up something cool or **meaningful**. You can use your imagination to imagine anything you want.

When you imagine how you want things to be, it's called **creative visualization**.

How does this work? The keyword is "visualize." Let's say you're invited to a **party** next week and you usually find yourself standing **alone** in a corner or just feeling **awkward**. This time, before the party, visualize yourself talking with the other people, **sharing** what's on your mind, joining the conversation. See yourself **laughing** and having a good time. This can help make it easier for you to do it for **real**.

Or, let's say you're looking to **hook up** with that guy or girl you've been admiring from a **distance**. Visualize yourself approaching him or her—what you will say, what **expression** you have on your face, what you're wearing, where you are, anything you can think of. Imagine how he or she will react. Make it **positive**. When you make your move, things will not go exactly how you imagined, but you should feel more **relaxed** and **confident**.

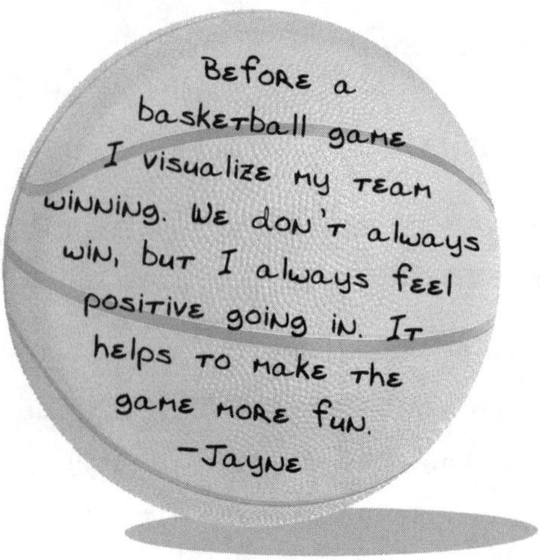
Before a basketball game I visualize my team winning. We don't always win, but I always feel positive going in. It helps to make the game more fun.
—Jayne

My foot said WHAT?!

Sometimes our **bodies** say more about us than our **words**. In fact, our bodies can have a **language** all their own. Do you have any idea what your body might be saying about you to **everyone** who sees you?

We don't have to let our bodies give away our insecurities—the **insecurities** we all have to some degree. We also don't want our bodies to say, "OMG, I love you!" or "Please be my **friend**!" too soon. We can teach our **bodies** a new language so we can **create** the impression we want to make.

When trying to make new friends or **catch** that guy or girl's **eye**, the most obvious thing to **AVOID** in your body's **vocabulary** is "downcast eyes." Not meeting someone's eyes can mean any number of things, but in this case, it just **SHOUTS** that you're not interested in making contact. And a wandering gaze might mean you've got **better** places to be and more **interesting** people to talk to. (If you do, move on!) So, definitely look your new potential "friend" in the eye, but don't make your gaze too intense. **Staring** at someone like that can creep them out!

It's not just your **eyes** that have a lot to say, it's also your **head**. Chin too high, and you may give the impression that you're overly **confident**. Too low, and you may give the message that you're **shy** or lacking confidence. It's hard to say exactly what's right, so just keep your **shoulders** and back **straight** and your head and chin should fall into their natural position.

Also, be aware of the **distance** between you and the other person. Too close at the start and you're a space invader; too **far** and you're unapproachable.

When you cross your **arms**, your body may be saying that you want to keep your distance. Yeah, it's **comfortable**, but it's best to avoid doing it when you first meet some-

Jayne, what's my body saying when it burps? –Jon

one. Better to put your hands in your **pockets** if you don't know what to do with them. If you want to **appear** open and **approachable**, avoid **hiding** behind objects like the pillows on a couch or holding your textbooks against your chest.

Just the truth.... That you're gross!
—Jayne

So, just what was it your foot was saying? Check out the body-language chart below to find out.

WHAT YOU DID	WHAT YOUR BODY SAID*
Walked briskly toward someone	"I know you're going to want to know me."
Let out a big ol' yawn	"Can you be any more boring?"
Put your hands on your hips	"Oh, yeah? Well, listen to this!"
Slapped your forehead	"How could I be so dumb?"
Arms open, palms up, shoulders relaxed	"I'm sincere and trustworthy."
Leaned back in your chair	"I'm relaxed and having fun!"
Started biting your nails	"You're making me nervous!"

*Things like facial expressions, emotions, and intent also come into play. So keep in mind that your body could be saying something else!

WHAT YOU DID	WHAT YOUR BODY SAID*
Tapped your foot	"I'm waiting, but not very patiently!"
Rolled your eyes	"Whatever!"
Licked your lips a lot	"I think you might kiss me!" ★
Titled your head	"Oh, you're sooo interesting!"
Blinked frequently (aka batted eyelashes)	"I am really into you."
Leaned forward	"We're going to be great friends."
Legs crossed, foot bobbing	"Let's get on with it already!"

*See page 33.

★ Hold on!
Maybe I'm just licking my lips cause they're chapped. —Jayne

LMAO!
-Jon

Let's Get Conversing!

We can't let our **bodies** do all the talking. Eventually, we've gotta open our **mouths** and say something **interesting** to start a **conversation** and make a **lasting** impression.

Hi, hey, and **what's up**? go only so far. What comes next? Introducing yourself **helps** and asking questions that are **open-ended** helps too. What do we mean by "open-ended"? Questions that can't be answered with a simple **yes** or **no** or a single word—those are **dead-end** questions, real conversation **stoppers**. Instead of asking, "What TV show do u like?" you can ask, "**Why** do u like that show?" Get the **idea**?

Chatterbox?
Maybe u never run outta stuff 2 say. But not everyone's like that. You can help by asking Qs and giving others something to chat about.

Getting other **people** to talk about themselves is a great way to help you (and them) feel more **relaxed**. The more you get to know someone, the **easier** it will be for you to talk about yourself. (Of course, some people have noooo **problem** talking about themselves! If you're one of them, be sure to give other people a chance to **talk** too!)

If you usually find yourself feeling like the **outsider** in a **group** of people, listen to what they're saying. Are they talking about a sporting **event** you didn't see or a TV show that's on the night you watch something else? Figure out what interests other people share and consider watching that **show** or catching the next sporting event, or whatever. This way, you can **join** in on the conversation next time.

Don't get us wrong. We're not saying you should change your **interests** just to fit in. We're suggesting you **try** some of the things other people talk about to see if they interest you. If not, maybe you'll want to find a **crowd** that more closely shares your interests—whatever they may be.

One way to be more comfortable talking to people you wouldn't normally approach is by **practicing** what you're gonna say. You don't have to rehearse your lines like a play—real life doesn't work that way. Just have some open-ended **Qs** available to you that can keep the conversation moving along.

Andy finally approached that new girl in our bio class. Here's how the **conversation** might have gone if we hadn't coached him the day before:

Andy: Hi.
New girl in bio: Hey.
Andy: I'm Andy.
New girl in bio: Oh. Hi.
Andy: You're new here.
New girl in bio: Yeah.
Andy: Umm, well, see ya around.
New girl in bio: Yeah, see ya.

Since Andy's a little shy around girls, he might have **screwed up** his first encounter with the new girl in bio if he didn't think (at least a little) about what he would say **beforehand**. Here's how the conversation really went:

Andy: Hi, I'm Andy. And you are?
New girl in bio: Hey, my name's Claudia.
Andy: Nice to meet you, Claudia. How do you like it here so far?

Claudia*: It's not bad. It's a bit different.

Andy: Yeah, what's different about it?

Claudia: Well, when I lived in the city, everything was so close, but here it's all so far away.

Andy: Nah, the mall's just 10 minutes away. Lots of my friends hang out there. Wanna come with me after school?

Claudia: Sure, that would be great.

Andy: Awesome! I'll ask Jon and Jayne to come too.

*AKA "the new girl in bio"

Thanks for the **invite**, Andy! Of course, if Claudia wasn't into him, she wouldn't have agreed to hang out with him, but if he hadn't asked, he would have never known. Andy took a **chance**. That's really what making new friends is all about: taking chances. It can be a little **nerve-wracking** when we risk rejection and failure, can't it? That's why we need to find courage. In fact, that's the keyword: **Courage**. Need a bit of it? See "Courage, Confidence, and Charisma" on page 41.

In the meantime, here are some dead-end questions with their open-ended **counterparts**.

Dead-End Qs	Open-Ended Qs
Where are you from?	What's it like where you're from?
Have you seen any good movies lately?	What did you think of the last movie you saw?
Have you ever done something crazy?	What's the craziest thing you ever did?
Do you like to shop?	What do you like best about the mall?
Do you think there's such a thing as a perfect date?	How would you describe the perfect date?
Did you work over the summer?	What did you do this summer?
Did you like the concert?	What was the best part of the concert?

How many **more** do you think you can come up with? Make your own list of open-ended questions. The **possibilities** are practically **endless.**

Have an answer of your own for any Qs you ask!

WHERE DO U STAND?

If you had to **choose** just one, which quality would you rate as being most **important** . . . in a **bf/gf**? . . . in a **friend**?

Would it be style, looks, sense of humor, intelligence, kindness, or **something else** entirely?

Go to **jonandjayne.com**, click on SURVEYS, and see where you (& others) stand in the grand 7F scheme.

Three C's

COURAGE, CONFIDENCE, AND *Charisma*

Charisma is this girl we know, and she's got a lot of it. **Everyone** wants to know her and be around her. She's friendly, **fascinating**, and interested in what other people have to say. Making new **friends** is no problem for her. She has a lot of good ideas and she **thrives** in new situations. Everything about life is exciting for her, and she meets new **challenges** head-on.

Not all of us are like Charisma. What's she got that some of us haven't got? **Courage** and **confidence**. In other words, a healthy dose of self-esteem. There's that keyword: **self-esteem**. We hear about it all the time. But what does it really mean? What does it mean to us?

Self-esteem is said to be high or low, seeming to suggest that either we **believe** in ourselves or we don't. We shouldn't forget that there's a **middle ground** too. We may have a healthy self-esteem in some areas, and in other areas it may be a little too low. For example, some of us might do **well** in school but **bomb** in social situations, or vice versa.

To figure out where you are on the self-esteem **scale**, think about how you **describe** yourself. Are the words you use positive, negative, or somewhere in **between**? Are there areas of your life you'd like to work on or things about yourself that you need to **accept**? Can you play up your positives a bit and let the negatives take a backseat?

Whatever the case may be, there's no doubt about it: you can **succeed**; we all can. Self-esteem is built one step at a time. And when we have good self-esteem, we gain **respect** for ourselves. When we respect ourselves, it makes it easier for us to put ourselves out there and take **chances**. We know that not everything is going to turn out in our **favor** (and we may even fail miserably!), but having good self-esteem also lets us know that's okay too. There will **always** be ups and downs!

Taking chances requires courage. It's something that we ALL have **somewhere** inside of us. Lots of things in life take **courage**, some more than others. Look inside yourself to find the courage you need to face whatever **challenges** your life is dealing you.

When you have courage, you will likely come across to people as being more **confident**—and you may even feel it. And when you present yourself that way, **people** are more likely to want to get to know you. You may even seem more **attractive** and more **approachable**, like Charisma. Here's what she has to say:

Some people are born with charisma. But I was born "Charisma." My friends think I have it soooo easy and that people are just naturally attracted to me. But just like everyone else, sometimes I'm really afraid. I'm afraid I'll be rejected, afraid I'll look stupid or say something dumb. And, believe me, I totally have! The only difference between me and someone who doesn't take any chances is that I don't let my fears stop me. I have the courage to face the consequences—even if I end up falling flat on my face!

If you can find your

COURAGE

the strength to face
your fears or difficulties

and your

CONFIDENCE

your faith in yourself
and your abilities

as well as your

Charisma

what makes you
appealing to others

you'll build your

Self-esteem

the belief you have
in yourself

Eric's Story

Putting Yourself Out There

When I first started middle school, I wasn't popular at all. I didn't really have a lot of friends and girls didn't really like me. One day, I just decided I was going to become popular. I was going to put myself out there. I started hanging out at all the cool places like the movie theater and the mall. I think being funny helped a lot. I have a good sense of humor, so I'm always cuttin' jokes and making people laugh. It makes people want to hang out with me.

It wasn't long after that that the girls started checkin' me out. I decided I just had to walk up to the girls I wanted to know and start talking, making conversation. This worked out pretty well and it just got easier. The more people who knew me, the more people wanted to know me.

Another way to become popular, at least for me, is to be a little on the crazy side—like olleing over a 3-foot gap and landing on my back. It hurt a little, but it sure was funny! Also, to get popular, I checked out what everyone was wearing. Girls pay more attention to brand names, but you still gotta dress right.

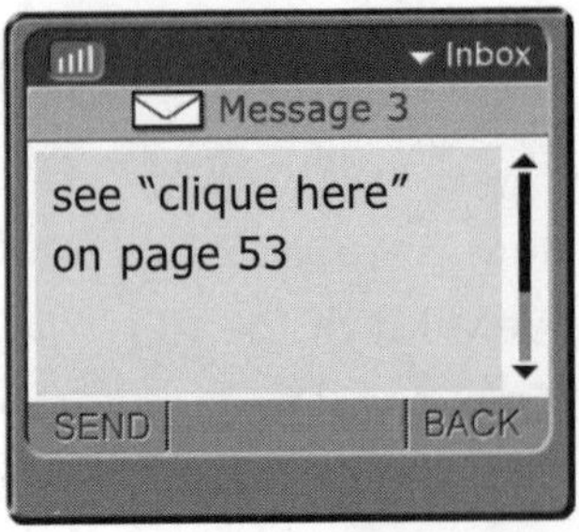

When it comes to friends, it's important to find your "crowd." For example, if you don't like black hair and dark eyeliner, don't hang with the "Goths." You have to be comfortable with the people you're hanging with.

As far as the ladies go, one way to get them is to be confident in yourself (and maybe a little cocky). You have to listen to what girls say, and this is the hardest part because they can talk FOREVER! This is the main thing: don't just pretend to listen.

You have to really listen because they will quiz you on what they say.

I think that what being popular is really about is having the courage to be true to yourself, your beliefs, and what you want to achieve in life. Trying to become popular shouldn't control you—you should just have fun with it. And don't expect to become popular overnight. It takes time and effort. It took me two years!

Eric D.

Eric's advice isn't half bad. It's great that he had the courage to "put himself out there." His crazy skateboard stunt may not have been so clever, but at least he got a good laugh out of it from the crowd . . . and was able to laugh about it himself.

The thing he said about dressing right for the crowd is probably true, but having brand-name clothes shouldn't be the focus. Sometimes, you can check out the brand-name catalogs and buy the same non-brand styles for less **$**.

If people only want to know you because you wear expensive clothing, chances are they just aren't worth the effort.

Eric gets extra points from me for figuring out the ladies. I agree that girls can talk way too much. That's why the keyword here is blabbermouth.

–Jon

Oh come on! Last night on the phone you went on for 15 minutes about the game! I couldn't get one word in. Guys can talk way too much too!

–Jayne

I guess you're right, but the keyword is still blabbermouth. It's the last keyword, and I like it. Besides, you owe me for 7F.

–Jon

OK, then, we're even . . . for now. ;)

–Jayne

Kait's Story

Got a Pen?

Making friends can be really tricky if you're shy, and when I first meet people, I admit I get self-conscious and nervous. I know that if I want to make friends I have to find the courage to take some chances. Nothing bad could possibly happen, could it?

When I started 9th grade, I was transferred to a new school—a private, all-girls school. On top of that, I had to wear a uniform, so I couldn't even express myself through my style! Still, I thought I would be able to handle it.

First day there, all the students met in the auditorium to get their homeroom assignments. It seemed like everybody was smart and outgoing. I just didn't feel like I fit in. I was stuck thinking about the negatives, and I was really nervous.

When I got my homeroom assignment, I felt a little better since there was a smaller crowd now. I still felt awkward because I didn't know anybody. I sat behind this girl Jen (we were in alphabetical order, so I didn't really have a choice). I thought for a second about how I could introduce myself to her. I didn't want to use the usual, "Hi, I'm Kait," but I knew I had to say something.

So, I tapped her on the shoulder and said, "Hey, do you have a pen I could borrow?" It didn't matter that I had a pen in my book bag. It was a great way to break the ice.

She said, "Sure!"

When she handed me the pen, she introduced herself. Then we started talking. I told her that I was new at the school and asked her what it was like there. We ended up having a pretty long conversation before the bell rang, and I had made my first friend at a new school.

I was so happy when she asked me to have lunch with her. I was relieved that I didn't have to worry about sitting alone. I had a friend, and all because I asked for a pen!

Kait R.

It's great that Kait was able to make a friend by simply asking to borrow a pen! Of course, it's not always that easy.

We know this girl, Karen, who asked the girl sitting in front of her for her phone number so she could call her for school assignments if she was absent. (It was Karen's first day at a new school.) The girl was really stuck up and rolled her eyes. "Ask somebody else," she said with an attitude. Karen was humiliated! Kait was lucky that Jen was a friendly person—clearly not everyone is.

Work up the courage to speak to a lot of different people to find someone you click with, and be prepared for some rejection. It sucks, but it's normal.

Fitting In

Punk? Biker? Nerd? Poser? Artist? Skater? Jock? Loner? Geek? Cheer-leader? Band kid? Floater? Surfer? Gamer? Goth? Wanna-be? Dancer?

Clique Here

We have an amazing **circle** of friends, and we're always doing stuff **together**, like going to the mall or having lunch as a group or just **hanging out**.

We're always on the **lookout** for **new** friends, and we don't care much if they look like us, dress like us, or act like us, as long as they're **cool** people.

What makes a person **cool**? Is it what they **wear**? What talents they have? What they **like** to do? How they act?

For us, it's the whole **package**. For others it may be something very specific. Pretty much **everyone** is looking for something that's important to them in a friend or group of friends.

Inbox
Message 4
sometimes 1 close friend is better than a whole clique
SEND
BACK

Sometimes it's **tough** figuring out where you really fit in within the grand **scheme** of cliques. Sometimes a clique is so tight you need a crowbar to get in. Sounds like a lot of **work**. But if you take it one person at a time (instead of approaching the whole group), it'll give you a chance to get to know them as **individuals**. This makes it possible for you to find out what they're really like beneath the **surface**. It will also make it **easier** to become part of the **group**—if you ultimately decide that crowd's for **you**.

If you are part of an "**exclusive**" clique, you and your friends may be limiting yourselves **socially**. Life is usually more **interesting** when you have many **different** experiences with different people. After all, isn't **variety** the spice of life? **Kick it up**!

Check out the "Which-Crew-R-U?" Quiz on jonandjayne.com

Joseph's story

All Roads Lead to Rome

I've been a member of the Italian Club since sixth grade. I'm in eleventh now. A few of the people in the club are my good friends. We hang out together on the weekends and at lunch and after school. My friends aren't limited to just people in the Italian club, so I wouldn't consider us a clique, but it's a good feeling to be part of something bigger than just myself.

Our club just got back from a tour of Italy. We had an amazing time! There was so much to do and see, and it was great being able to experience this with people my age. I've been to Italy with my family and even though I had a great time then too, being with my friends made the trip really exciting.

We began in Rome, where we saw the Sistine Chapel and the Coliseum. Then we went on to Naples, then to Florence (where Leonardo DaVinci once lived). We visited Pisa and saw the Leaning Tower. We got to spend part of the day on a beach in Jesolo on the Adriatic Sea. Venice was really cool, but the water was gross. Then Verona (the setting for *Romeo and Juliet*), Lake Como, Milan (where I bought a leather wallet), and Turin.

All along we were goofing around and taking pictures and just having a really great time. Our chaperones were really cool too and had as much fun as we did. We had some arguments here and there, but it was nothing we couldn't work out.

The food was *delicioso!* We ate so much. Lunch was my favorite meal of the day. The people were really friendly, and we got to converse with them in Italian.

I can't imagine not having gone on this trip. There was never any question that I would join the Italian Club since my whole family is from Italy. But even if someone's not from Italy, even if

• READER SURVEY •

JMHT

We care about your opinions! Take a minute to fill out HCI's online Reader Survey at http://survey.hcibooks.com, and you'll get a coupon toward future book purchases and a special gift available only online! Or you can mail this card back to us.

First Name *MI.* *Last Name*

Street Address *City* *State* *Zip*

E-mail address

1. Are you . . .

❒ Female? ❒ Male?

2. How old are you?

❒ 8 or younger ❒ 9–12

❒ 13–16 ❒ 17–20 ❒ 21+

3. Did you receive this book as a gift?

❒ Yes ❒ No

4. Where do you usually buy books? (choose one)

❒ Book Club/Mail Order

❒ Bookstore

❒ Internet

❒ Price Club such as Costco

❒ Retail Store such as Target

5. What type of magazine do you like best? (choose one)

❒ Celebrity News

❒ Fashion & Advice

❒ Gaming

❒ Music News

❒ Sports

❒ Religious

6. What type of book do you like best? (choose one)

❒ Fiction

❒ Self-Improvement

❒ Reality/Memoir

❒ Sports

❒ Series books

7. What's your favorite website?

NO POSTAGE
NECESSARY
IF MAILED
IN THE
UNITED STATES

BUSINESS REPLY MAIL

FIRST-CLASS MAIL PERMIT NO 45 DEERFIELD BEACH, FL

POSTAGE WILL BE PAID BY ADDRESSEE

The Jon & Jayne Doe Series
3201 SW 15th Street
Deerfield Beach FL 33442-9875

they aren't Italian (or whatever nationality), clubs like these can offer us the chance for great experiences. *Ciao!*

Joseph C.

What a trip that must've been! Joseph is really lucky to have gotten to participate in such an amazing adventure with people he feels connected to. We can all reach out for those kinds of connections.

A school club, like a foreign-language club, gives us the chance to share experiences with like-minded people. School clubs aren't cliques, and they don't exclude anyone who has a sincere interest in the subject. Although we might not hang out after school and on the weekends with everyone in the club, there's a pretty good chance we'll develop good friendships through the club.

Whether it's the drama club, math club, foreign-language club, chess club, bowling team, band, or whatever you're interested in, you'll find people who share your interests and who will most likely accept you, and you might just find yourself going on great adventures or reaching new heights alongside them.

Taylor's Story

The Black Sheep Squadron

About two years ago, my friend and I were getting pushed around a lot. So we decided it was time to toughen up. We and three of our friends started a group called the Black Sheep Squadron (BSS). The name itself was pioneered from the bombing squadrons of WWII.

We don't consider ourselves a clique or a gang, we just hang out together. We don't do anything illegal like steal things or start fights, but we will defend ourselves if we have to. Most people don't realize what we have going on, because we're just a small group of five. But being part of this group makes us feel more secure and we don't get pushed around anymore.

Taylor W.

As the saying goes, there's safety in numbers. Getting pushed around by a group of bullies—or even a gang—can be really scary and upsetting. Gang violence and bullying are two very real things that concern most of us these days. Protecting ourselves by fighting back can result in suspension from school or could result in serious injury, so we hope Taylor and his friends defend themselves through their words and other nonviolent actions.

We think everyone should become involved in some type of violence-prevention program at their school. If there aren't any programs like that at your school, it would be a good idea to talk to your teachers about starting one.

If you do find yourself in a conflict, try to talk your way out of it and walk away. If you really feel physically threatened by someone, tell your parents and report that person to school authorities right away. If you end up in a seriously threatening situation and there's no adult to turn to for help, grab your cell phone and call the police.

Taking matters into your own hands could easily backfire. You might think it'll be worse if you tell on someone, but the consequences of not telling could be disastrous.

We're going to talk about dealing with bullies (and gangs) in Issue #3, *Jon & Jayne's Guide to Getting Through School (Mostly Intact).*

We take Kenpo classes twice a week, but we've never had to use the skills we've learned in a real-life situation. We're instructed not to use our self-defense skills unless seriously threatened with bodily harm. But just knowing how to defend ourselves against a real unarmed attacker has done a lot for our confidence. Not only that, our Kenpo classes are actually lots of fun and keep us in pretty good shape!

Betania's Story

The Battle of the Cliques

Our world is a hard place to live in—sort of like a battlefield, where we're all soldiers just trying to survive, trying to figure out which side we're on. This isn't easy. We're battling for love and acceptance, but there are so many boundaries. If we cross them, we may be viewed as an enemy or a comrade. It's hard to tell which it'll be. In school, these boundaries are formed by cliques, which can help us fit in, but they can also make us feel like outsiders and even destroy our self-confidence.

I've felt what it's like to be in a clique. It's amazing when you get to school and expect it to be just another typical, almost perfect, day with your friends. You get there and they're laughing and telling jokes and you just join in the conversation and talk to everybody. This is where you belong. At lunch, you sit with these amazing people. They love being with you, and you're never alone, not ever. You always have someone to tell what's on your mind. Even if it is just a quick trip to the bathroom or your locker, they're there for you. When you leave school for the day, everyone hugs and makes plans for going out that night. Seems like life couldn't get any better, huh?

I've also felt what it's like not to be part of a group. The first day at a new school, there was nobody I could share my amazing summer vacation with. In class, when group projects were assigned, I'd end up doing an individual project. At lunch, I'd sit alone while others shared a big table of friends. On the bus, I'd sit quietly, staring out the window, wondering why life seemed so cruel. I felt hurt and scared deep inside.

It seems right that people should team up with people who are most like them. When they pick friends, they pick the ones they most relate to. Sometimes, though, it goes further than that. They become so teamed up that they won't let anyone else into their clique. This makes it really hard for new students. They try to become friends, but the cliques are so well formed and too exclusive to let in any newcomers. Only a chosen few are permitted to enter. The ones who are rejected feel isolated and alone, thinking they don't belong. School can become a dreadful experience for people who are unaccepted, who have to eat lunch alone, and who feel so out of place that they wonder if they'll ever fit in.

In a lot of ways, people who form cliques are creating their own worlds—different worlds for different people. They separate themselves, finding refuge among others of their own kind. They don't learn how to live alongside people who are different from them. They create their own territories and don't allow others to safely cross the boundaries. That's part of what makes a teenager's life like a battlefield. The casualties are those who are made to feel like they belong to "no-man's" land.

Betania C.

Have you ever been the outsider? If so, you know what Betania's talking about. Feeling left out can really hurt and make a person wonder what's wrong with them.

Sometimes, outsiders create their own "one-person clique," and don't let anyone cross their boundaries cause they're afraid to get hurt. In other cases, some people are just really shy and find it difficult to approach others. And in still other cases, a person is rejected for not being enough like the others, even though shyness has nothing to do with it. And of course someone may be an outsider just because they are new to the area.

Whatever the case may be, it's usually not much fun to be an outsider. Maybe you could approach someone like that and learn what he or she is all about. And if you are that person, you don't have to be alone. Start small by joining an after-school club or sport.

Sometimes, we'll approach someone who is all alone to help them feel welcome. Occasionally we get rejected, but sometimes we discover a new friend or help someone gain the confidence to make other friends.

Ashley's Story

Not for Me

As I stood in the doorway of my new school, I looked around at all the people waiting in the main hall, not knowing who to talk to first or who I'd fit in with. I told myself to just walk straight in.

It didn't take me very long to realize that there are all types of cliques in my school—many of them come from the activities they do, like the jocks and bodybuilders, cheerleaders and preps, dance and step, chorus and drama, head-bangers and rockers, skaters and skanks, nerds and geeks. Then it all comes down to what "color" you are: Brazilian, Puerto Rican, Asian, Black, or White.

I don't believe in cliques. It's usually all about stereotyping, prejudice, and discrimination. People should be who they want to be without being judged. Unfortunately, in high school, lots of people think they should only be friends with people who are the same and that anyone who's the slightest bit different is conceited or a freak.

School is another world—cliques make it that way. I simply say belonging to a clique isn't for me. I talk 2 everybody.

Ashley K.

Ashley sounds pretty cool—we bet she made a lot of different friends at her new school. It's true that we can't be friends with everybody, but we don't have to limit ourselves to people who wear a certain style of clothing or who look a certain way.

There's nothing wrong with hanging with people we relate to, and when we start at a new school, of course we're gonna want to find people who have similar interests. But there's a lot to be said for learning about people—and even becoming friends with people—who are not necessarily like us. That's how we become more worldly and open-minded—two really awesome traits.

ACQUIRING ACQUAINTANCES versus Finding Friends

Sometimes we'll really **click** w/ someone and become friends almost instantly—and it's like we've always known that person. But most friendships don't happen overnight. It takes **time.**

Potential friends usually begin as acquaintances. We avoid **confusing** them w/ our good friends—people we share almost everything with. This is because it's **hard** to tell how much you can really trust someone you don't **know** all that well. How long it takes b4 you consider someone your **friend** is up to your gut feelings.

Being able to **trust** someone is **huge**! It's not always easy trying to determine who you can really trust. To help you **figure** it out, ask yourself these Qs. If you answer **NO** to any of them, think seriously about **sharing** your personal info and **secrets** with that person.

- Do you truly like this person, really?
- Does he/she respect who you are?
- Does he/she share your views on things that are very important to you?
- Has he/she ever confided in you?
- As far as you know, does he/she keep other people's secrets?
- Are you pretty sure this person has never lied to you or talked behind your back?
- Do your gut feelings tell you that this person is trustworthy?

These aren't **fail-safe** questions. You may answer **YES** to every one and still end up being betrayed. Or you may answer **NO** to every one and be **wrong** about how much you could trust that person. Like most things in this **wacky** world, trusting **people** involves taking chances.

> "You may be deceived if you trust too much,
> but you will live in torment if you do not trust enough."
>
> —Frank Crane (some guy who was born in 1861 and died in 1928 and wrote some thought-provoking stuff)

The LOVE Broker

Do you think it's OK to be the go-between for a good friend who's **crushing** on someone you know? Last week, we were trying to decide if one of us should tell Rick that Kelly's **totally** into him. Even if Kelly wanted us to, was it cool to be a "**love broker**"? Here's what we decided:

It usually won't **hurt**, and sometimes it might even **help.** Kelly decided that she would absolutely never in a **zillion** years tell Rick that she **likes** him, but she wanted him to **know** and she wanted to know if he liked her back. She practically **begged** us to say something. We decided Jon would be the one to tell Rick, since they're on the soccer **team** together.

I told Rick that Kelly is really into him. At first he didn't even know who I was talking about. Then he said he didn't really know her. He said he guessed she was sort of cute, but then said that he likes someone else. I told Jayne and Jayne told Kelly.

I told Kelly that Rick said he doesn't really know her. I also said that he likes someone else. I didn't tell her the other stuff, like that he said she was only "sort of cute" or that he didn't even know who Jon was talking about at first. I left that stuff out. Kelly was really disappointed. She still likes Rick, but at least now she realizes that she doesn't know him very well either.

♥ ♥ ♥

Well, it didn't work out for Kelly and Rick, but when Jesse told Kelly that Kenny has a **crush** on her, Kelly said she thought Kenny was **sort of cute.** They're going out for a slice of pizza tomorrow afternoon. So sometimes it **works** out, other times it doesn't.

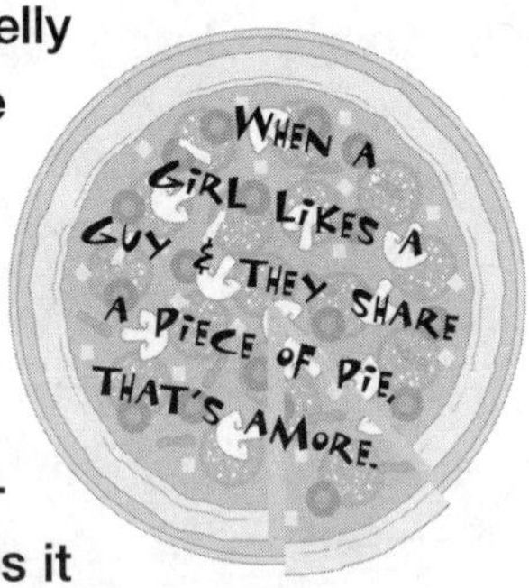
WHEN A GIRL LIKES A GUY & THEY SHARE A PIECE OF PIE, THAT'S AMORE.

If you're going to be the **go-between**, there are some things you should know. First of all, **make sure** the following 2 conditions are in place before you open your **mouth**:

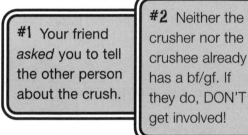

#1 Your friend *asked* you to tell the other person about the crush.

#2 Neither the crusher nor the crushee already has a bf/gf. If they do, DON'T get involved!

Once those 2 conditions have been met, make sure you follow these 4 rules:

#1 Don't exaggerate how your friend feels and don't put words in your friend's mouth. State the case as briefly as possible.

#2 Don't make your friend out to be some psycho stalker.

#3 Don't have an ulterior motive. You must NOT have a crush on this person too. If you do, stay out of it.

#4 Don't make up things about your friend to get the other person interested. Represent him or her honestly.

If you ask a friend to tell someone how you feel, make sure you TOTALLY trust him or her.

Once you've done the **deed**, if you have good news, that's **awesome.** If not, try to break it to your friend as **gently** as possible. Be sensitive.*

Sure, the best **advice** is to tell your friend to tell the person he/she is crushing on **directly.** But, hey, this is **reality**, and sometimes it doesn't hurt to intervene—if you have **good intentions.**

* Yeah, EVEN if you'RE a guy!

Whoa, Jayne! I PRIDE myself on my xtraordinary sensitivity.

Oh pleeze, JON.

Wat?

He Said, She Said

So he said, "Jayne said you like me."

And she said, "Jayne said that?"

And he said, "That's what she said, is it true?"

And she said, "First tell me if what
Jon said is true."

And he said, "Jon said something?
What'd he say?"

And she said, "He said you like me."

And he said, "Jon said that?"

And she said, "Yeah, that's what he said."

And he said, "Yeah, what Jon said is true."

And she said, "Yeah, so's what Jayne said."

TRUTH

You've GOTTA Hear This...!

Rumor:
A story about a person that lacks truth or real proof.

Gossip:
To spread a rumor or share personal information about someone else.

Do you listen to **rumors**? We do, because it's hard not to when there are so many of them going around school! The **important** thing, though, is do we **believe** them? And do we **repeat** them? Do you? Has anyone ever started a rumor about **you**? Have you ever **started** a rumor about someone?

We call people who start rumors ***sleazemongers.*** We found this word in the thesaurus (really) under "**gossip**." It's a good word because many rumors can be very **hurtful**, so it's **sleazy** to start one.

Rumors can range from slightly embarrassing to seriously **damaging**. Here's an example of one **rumor** that screwed up a good **friendship** and a possible **relationship**:

Rachel heard that her crush, Paul, and her best friend, Paige, kissed under the bleachers during PE two days ago. She heard it from one of the girls on the track team, who heard it from a band kid, who heard it from one of the jocks, who happens to be dating the best friend of the girl who started the rumor.

(Turns out, this girl is Felicia and she has a crush on Paul too. She's seen Rachel and Paul flirting and decided that she could divert Rachel's attention away from Paul by getting her into a fight w/ Paige and getting her to question whether Paul really liked her.)

Believing the rumor to be true, Rachel freaked on Paige. When Paige finally convinced Rachel the rumor wasn't true, she got mad at Rachel for even believing it.

Meanwhile, Felicia made her move on Paul. Since Rachel suddenly wasn't speaking to him (he couldn't figure out why), Paul decided to go for it. But when he heard the rumor about him & Paige, he soon figured out it was Felicia who started the whole thing. He dumped her.

When Rachel found out that Paul hooked up w/ Felicia, she was really hurt and wouldn't accept his apology. Rachel and Paige finally made up, but their friendship was strained. It took them a while to rebuild the trust.

This rumor might have seemed "**innocent**" on the surface, but it really **changed** things for those involved. Rumors can be a lot more **malicious** than this too. But even if they're not, even if it's only something like "Oh, that girl is crazy," rumors can **color** the way somebody looks at somebody else.

- **What to do if you hear a rumor?** Don't just believe it. Don't spread it. Let the rumor die w/ you. Also, don't let it change your opinion of the person it's about. Make up your own mind about someone by getting to know him/her.

- **What to do if you hear a rumor about a close friend?** Tell your friend what you've heard, but not like "Hey, I heard what you did." Instead say something like, "I know this probably didn't really happen, but I heard . . ." And then figure out together if the rumor is serious enough to try to dispel.

- **What to do if you hear a rumor about something that could be dangerous?** Tell someone like a parent, a trusted teacher, or a counselor. Even if it's only partially true, or just somebody venting, you're better off telling than waiting for disaster to strike.

- **What to do if the rumor is about you?** Decide how important it is to you. If the rumor has the potential to damage one of your relationships, speak to that person before the rumor gets back to him or her or explain that the rumor he or she heard simply isn't true. If it's something you can laugh off, then laugh.

- **What if the rumor about you is true?** What if you really were kissing your bff's bf or gf under the bleachers? Well, if that's the case, you're on your own. Good luck!

RUMOR RECON & RECOVERY

- When you first hear a rumor about yourself or a friend, take the **B3C** stance: Be **C**alm, **C**ool, and **C**ollected, yeah, even if you're fuming inside—no matter how hard it might be!
- Ask a question like "Who said that?" or "Where did you hear that?" but first say something like "You've got to be kidding—that's totally ridiculous!"
- Every time you hear the rumor, laugh about it, and say something like, "Yeah, right, like that would ever happen."
- Go straight to the source and ask the person who started the rumor if they somehow got the story confused. Always maintain your B3C stance. Act like the person made a big mistake and offer to help him or her make it right.
- If the rumor is about an illegal or dangerous activity, speak to an adult or school authority as soon as possible to resolve the issue.
- If the rumor is about you and someone else, speak to the other person privately, face to face, to clear the air and safeguard your relationship.
- Just be yourself. Some people will believe what they've heard no matter what you do or say, so the best thing to do is just go about your life like you never heard it. Your actions will win out over any words of protest.

JD GaTEr 110: hey jayne i heard a rumor about u today on the bus

JaynE SaYs 611: oh really . . . what?

JD GaTEr 110: heard u r crushing on someone whose name starts with j

JaynE SaYs 611: lol oh please. . . . don't listen to rumors!

JD GaTEr 110: you're not gonna say that's totally ridiculous?

JaynE SaYs 611: i'm not gonna say anything

JD GaTEr 110: that's a first

JaynE SaYs 611: buh-bye

JD GaTEr 110: wait!

JaynE SaYs 611: c u 2moro in homeroom

JaynE SaYs 611 has signed off.

JD GaTEr 110 has signed off.

Samantha's Story

Sydney, Soccer, and Me

A girl named Sydney became my friend, but we were not friends at first sight. In fact, it took us about a year or two to really get to know each other. I once heard from a girl in my neighborhood that Sydney can sometimes say mean things to her friends and was a negative person. So, I stayed away from her. Another girl I know said that Sydney was a "girly girl" and that although she played soccer she wasn't really good at it. Since I am a serious soccer player and consider myself to be a sporty kind of girl, I just figured we were not meant to be friends.

Recently, I realized that Sydney wasn't really mean. She was at a party that I went to. She was nice to me and acted like she wanted to be my friend. It was a nice surprise. Could that girl in my neighborhood be wrong? After the party, I didn't really see Sydney that much, but a couple weeks later, school soccer season came around. I tried out for the soccer team, and so did Sydney. I made the team as a goalie and Sydney made it as a defender.

A few weeks after tryouts the first game of the soccer season came around. Right before we were about to take the field, my soccer coach pulled me aside and said, "Sam, Sydney is going to be your best friend, she is your main defender, so you guys will be working together a lot."

I knew the first rumor I'd heard about Sydney wasn't true, but I still wasn't sure if she was good at soccer or not. So I was concerned about her being one of my key defenders.

At our first game, I was under pressure from the start. There were a lot of shots on goal and I did my best to save them. Suddenly, I spotted this enormous girl dribbling the ball toward my goalie box. She faked out several players who tried to stop her attack. All she had to do was get past me to score. She kept dribbling closer and closer and it seemed like this girl was going to plow right into me.

All of a sudden, out of nowhere, Sydney came sprinting back to help me. Although it seemed impossible to catch up to the attacking player, Sydney did it and cleared the ball out of the box, saving me from possibly being scored on or even injured!

"Thanks, Syd!" I shouted. "No problem," she replied with a huge smile.

From then on Sydney and I became the dynamic duo on and off the soccer field. And I learned a good lesson: Don't believe rumors. Get the facts about a person before you judge them. You might just get a friend out of it.

Samantha D.

Way to go, Sam and Sydney! Just goes to show that rumors we hear about a person shouldn't be taken seriously until we discover the truth for ourselves. We rest our case!

We bet you've got a **conundrum**—virtually all of us do. No, it's not a new deadly disease spread by infected purple-crested warblers. It's a **problem**, usually w/ a **complex** answer.

If you've got a conundrum, go to jonandjayne.com and click on CONUNDRUMS & SOLUTIONS. We'll put our heads together and try to help you (and other people who have the same problem) out w/ our "**solution**" in an upcoming issue.

We'll also check w/ **Dr. Toni** (see her bio on page 114) to be sure we're on the right track. Dr. Toni can be a bit **wordy**, but she's pretty **cool** and always has some good stuff 2 say.

But don't wait for us! If you've got a **serious** problem, talk to an **adult** you trust. Don't let your conundrum get the best of you. Find a **solution**!

Conundrums & Solutions

CONUNDRUM

I just **moved** from ID to NY, and I'm having a hard time getting used to it. My friends in Idaho were more **like me** than these New Yorkers. It's been a month already, and I haven't made any friends. I talk to some people, but we don't **hang out.** I go to the library at lunch so I don't have to sit alone. I always feel like the **odd person out.**

Kevin

SOLUTION

Ya know, people from NY aren't that **different** from people in ID. They might sound different, have different expressions, and have a slightly different **culture**, but we're all sharing the same space. Deep down, we all have the same **hopes** and **fears**. When you give some of those NYers a chance, you'll see you have a lot more **in common** than you think.

It sounds to us like you already have some **acquaintances**, so why not take the **first step** and ask if they wanna hang out with you one nite. It takes a while to **build** friendships, but if you make an effort, it'll happen.

BTW, don't hide in the library! You'll never **make friends** that way—unless you run into someone else who's hiding in the library too. Go to the library because you want or need to read or study, not because you're **embarrassed** to be seen alone. Lunch time is the time to **socialize** in school. Chances are, someone will strike up a **conversation** with you. If not, why don't you try it? Check out "Let's Get Conversing" on page 35.

As for your friends in ID, **keep in touch** thru e-mail, texting, IMs, and phone calls. Idaho might seem really far away right now, but it's not going anywhere.

Dr. Toni says:

It's true that people are more alike than they are different. Accents and cultural expressions do not really define a person. People relate based on characteristics like similar interests, hobbies, or shared experiences. If you enjoy such things as sports, music, or going out to dinner (which are universal), then you can likely develop social connections with people from anywhere in the country, or world, for that matter.

Do try starting a conversation with others and asking those with whom you have already spoken to get together after school. Sometimes what holds us back is fear. In order to confront your fear, take a risk and approach a social situation with assertiveness and confidence. Although you may not feel confident, fake it (this is my "fake it till you feel it" philosophy). You will see that people will want to hang out with you if you present yourself as someone who is friendly and open.

CONUNDRUM

There's this guy, Matt, who I'm totally **crushing** on, but he's a player. His last gf has a bad **reputation** and so did his gf before that. I've heard that he only dates girls who go all the way. He drops hints that he's into me, but how can I be **sure**? It seems like he flirts with **everyone**! How do I get this guy to be **mine**?

Kerry

SOLUTION

What do you like about Matt? What are his **positive** qualities? Do you know what he likes or dislikes, or **anything** about him other than his "notorious" reputation? If not, you don't really know him.

You can only get to know Matt by talking to him about **stuff that matters** to you and to him, and this takes time. Getting together with a group of friends is also a good way to get to **know** someone you're crushing on. When you see how he acts with other people, it can give you a good look into his personality to see if it's **compatible** with yours.

Once you get to know the **REAL** Matt, you can decide if he's someone you want to date.

Anyone who wants to hook up with you just to **have sex** with you isn't worth your time. If you think Matt's one of those people, he's totally **NOT** worth it. He's already been thru at least 2 gfs—don't be the third!

Remember, too, that just because you **hook up** with someone doesn't mean you have to get **physical.** Save that for someone **special** who you've dated for a long time and really **trust.** When you know w/o a doubt that you're ready and you're sure you both want an LTR (long-term relationship), that's the time to start considering that important **decision.**

Dr. Toni says:

I agree that you should get to know Matt as a person before deciding just how "into him" you are. I would suggest that you try to start a conversation with him, call him, text him, or IM him. If it turns out that he is interested in you, then I would be prepared to be confronted with his advances. It is very easy to get caught up in a moment and to lose sight of such things as sexually transmitted diseases and pregnancy. It is absolutely vital to recognize that these are REAL possibilities and to have a plan for protecting yourself. Ideally, speak to your mother or an aunt or other close adult to explore the idea of getting physical before taking that step. Of course it is always best to wait until you are older and in a better position to deal with any consequences. That being said, the reality is that some teenagers these days are experimenting. So, be smart about it. And understand that if sex is all a boy wants, then he may not be as interested in the relationship afterward. So be prepared to deal with the emotional strain the whole event may cause.

FOR MORE INFO ON THIS COMPLEX TOPIC, KEEP AN EYE OUT FOR ISSUE #4 JON & JAYNE'S GUIDE TO TEEN "FLINGS" ('N OTHER GUY/GIRL THINGS). . . . IF YOU HAVE QUESTIONS, DON'T 4GET TO TURN TO THE RESOURCES THAT ARE AVAILABLE TO YOU RIGHT NOW.

CONUNDRUM

Luke, my **best friend**, and his girlfriend, Josie, hooked up about 4 months ago. I think Josie's **really hot**, and whenever the three of us are together, I get totally **jealous**. I know I shouldn't feel this way, but I just can't help it. I think I'm going to go **crazy**! How should I go about telling Luke and Josie how I feel?

Carlos

SOLUTION

Sometimes we can't do much about how we feel. But we don't have to act on those feelings. If we do, the results could be **disastrous**! Anything you say about your crush on Josie could ruin your friendship with Luke.

What you should probably do is think about what it is you like about Josie. Okay, so she's hot. There are other **hot girls** out there, so that can't be the only thing you like about her. Does she have a good sense of **humor**? Is she smart? Does she like the same things you like? Try to pinpoint her positive qualities and then keep your eyes **wide open** for another girl (who doesn't have a boyfriend) who has those or similar qualities. Then make your move. You'll find someone of your own to **hook up** with!

In the meantime, limit the amount of time you spend with Luke and Josie. Don't be rude or vague about it, and don't cut them off completely. Just make plans with **other friends.**

Dr. Toni says:

While you can't help the way you feel, it is important to try to understand what is making you want Josie. It would be foolish to think that we can just go after anything we want in life without consequences. Since Luke is your best friend, you wouldn't want to hurt him by telling him that you have a crush on his girlfriend, or worse, by making advances at her.

This particular conundrum might need some further exploration with a counselor, because a lot is at risk and there may be underlying feelings contributing to your desire to be with Josie. For example, do you feel a competitiveness with Luke or an envy of him for any particular reason? Or, deep down, do you think that Josie has taken your best friend away from you? Or maybe you feel like you're not good enough because Josie is dating Luke and not you. Give yourself a chance to figure out the answers to these questions and work on your self-esteem.

CONUNDRUM

Lots of people at school think I'm a nerd because I'm really smart, but I want them to think of me as cool. What should I do?

Steven

SOLUTION

Being smart **IS** cool. And nerds these days are getting a lot more respect than they used to. If not for really smart people, we'd have no PCs, iPods, cell phones, etc. etc.—then where would we be?! Just go w/ it and don't try to be something you're not. If you want to expand your horizons, though, that's a different story. If the "cool" people are participating in certain activities that you find interesting, why not try your hand at them too? Will doing what they're doing make you cool? Don't know. Truth is, it's all in your head: You're only as cool as you think you are.

Dr. Toni says:

Sure, the PC answer is to say that being smart is cool (and it is!), but the reality is if you don't feel cool and it's important to you, you need to take some action.

You can gain the tools to be more assertive, more self-confident, and more outgoing by reading self-help books and practicing the strategies they suggest. Professional counseling is also an option. You can try wearing clothes that are in style and getting physically fit by working out at the gym or exercising regularly. You also might want to try an updated haircut.

You can do this all without sacrificing who you are inside. This *might* change the way other people perceive you. But what matters most is that you are true to yourself. If you strive to be the best that you can be, physically and mentally, you'll feel good about yourself—and that's what makes you cool.

The world belongs to the enthusiast who keeps cool.

—William McFee (1881–1966)*

*Did they even have cool people back then?

They had cool quotes.

BTW, what's an enthusiast?

Go Google it

VENT

When it comes to friends and crushes, what do we do when what we want conflicts with what our parents want? It's a tough call. Let's look at these sticky situations:

Michelle says:

"My parents are so lame! I'm not allowed to have a boyfriend until I'm 16. It's so totally unfair! How am I going to wait another year and a half?!"

SECRET: Michelle's not going to wait—she's meeting up with her crush this weekend w/o her parents knowing.

Meanwhile, Scott says:

"My mom and dad don't 'approve' of my new friends, but I really like hanging out with them. They can't pick my friends for me!"

SECRET: Scott's going to sneak out his window Saturday nite to go the "private" party his new friend Marshall is having.

Lots of us do stuff like this all the time, and lots of us get away w/ it. . . . But not always. Sometimes we can get ourselves into real **trouble**.

Before you think about doing anything you know your parents won't approve of, **consider** their rules and why they made them. They're usually for our safety and not just because our parents want to make our lives even **tougher** than they already are.

Do your parents' **rules** and **expectations** make it tough for you to be honest with them? Have you tried talking to them to explain your point of view? Can you try to come to a **compromise**? Like most things, it's easier said than done, but it is possible and it deserves a **chance**.

We know Michelle's **crush**, and he's not some Internet **psycho**. He's just a **regular** guy. Even though she's going behind her parents' back to meet up w/ him, she's letting her **friends** know where she'll be. And that's always a good idea.

As for Scott, that party at Marshall's is going to be **bad news**. Marshall's parents are out of town, and he has the key to the **liquor** cabinet. Scott's going to end up getting **wasted**, and when he tries to climb back into his window, he's going to fall and break his arm. Then, that's it for **football** this season.

Truth is, we keep a lot of **stuff** from our parents. If they knew every little thing about every **aspect** of our lives, they probably couldn't handle it. It's the **important** stuff that we need to talk to them about, things that have the **potential** to change our lives. When we absolutely can't talk to our parents, it helps to talk to an older brother or sister, a teacher, counselor, or someone else who can give us **objective** advice.

And, when all else **fails**, when we can't get our parents to understand how we feel, **venting** about how unfair we think they are helps to get some of the **negativity** out.

POINT TO PONDER

Why is it that other people's parents always seem so much cooler than our own?

Crystal's Story

Sneaking Around

When you're in your teens, it's hard to give in to your parents when you feel that their rules are unfair. We're trying to become adults and give up our "little kid" ways and move forward. My aunt and uncle raised me, not my parents, and I knew that if I disobeyed them, it was pure disrespect. So, if they told me I couldn't go to a party, wear a particular outfit, or whatever, I didn't argue and I didn't hold a grudge. I knew that someday I'd be able to do whatever I wanted to do. That was my attitude—until I met Alex, my first boyfriend.

Alex and I were from two different races. My aunt and uncle have old-fashioned beliefs and think that interracial dating is taboo. Still, I was falling headfirst for Alex. Alex and I would hang out on the weekends and talk for hours on the phone.

We kept our relationship secret from my family for five months. People on the streets often gave us weird looks, like *what are those two doing together? Don't they know they're too different?* I thought racism didn't exist anymore in America. Racist people are just ignorant, and they still exist, even here. Don't they know that the feeling of love is the same in every nation?

I sort of understand why my aunt and uncle wanted me to be with someone of my "own kind," but I have my own feelings and opinions and needed to do what felt right for me. Alex and I eventually broke up, but I wonder if we would still be together if people didn't judge our relationship. I don't regret the time Alex and I spent together—it was something I learned from. There's still a lot we have to do to raise awareness that we're all the same despite our differences.

Crystal G.

In the 21st century, you might think that dating someone who isn't the same race as you would not be such a big issue, that it wouldn't matter. But a lot of parents—and in Crystal's case, aunt and uncle—are against it. The same often goes for dating someone who isn't the same religion as you.

Crystal has a good point that the heart knows no boundaries, and lots of people find themselves faced with a true dilemma: they feel a true connection with someone they are forbidden to date. In some cases, they might date this person just to get attention from their parents.

If you're faced with this dilemma, ask yourself if you're dating someone you "shouldn't" just to get attention or if you really and truly like that person. If you decide that your feelings are real, you might want to see if you can resolve this particular conflict with your parents. Good luck!

Franklin's Story

My Agreement Plan

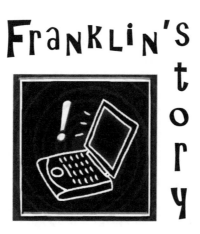

I've been living a rather hard life for a sixteen-year-old. My parents are as strict as can be. My brother was shot a few years ago as he was walking down the street . . . yup, just because of something he was wearing or because he was walking a certain way and some random guy didn't like it. It was a senseless act—and my brother was taken from my family for no reason.

After that my whole life changed. I was and still am the baby of the family, whether I like it or not. With an older brother and sister living out of state, I'm the only one left. After that horrific event, my parents wouldn't let me even leave the house for a while. I understood at first and I didn't even want to go out, but I started going stir crazy.

After a while, my mom started loosening up, but she was still stricter than most parents. So, I came up with an idea of making an "agreement plan" with my mom and dad. I confronted them about this "agreement plan" and told them what I had in mind. I suggested how about on Fridays and Saturdays I could go out as long as my mom knew exactly where I was in case of an emergency, and I would call to check in with her so she would know that I was okay. I even suggested a curfew of 9:30–10:00, even though this kind of upset me because all of my friends were allowed to stay out till 11, some even 12.

My parents were willing to go along with the plan, and I stick to it. I'm never late and I always make sure my parents know exactly what's going on. After what happened to my brother, I realize that it's important for my parents to know where I am. I understand that my parents care about me, love me, and just want me to be safe. And I appreciate that.

Franklin B.

Wow, Franklin. We're so sorry to hear about your brother. It can be a very scary and crazy world sometimes, and that's why it really does make sense to be sure all our bases are covered—where we are, who we're with, when we'll be home, and so on.

Our parents want to keep us safe, which is why they make the rules they do. Sometimes their rules may seem unfair or a little extreme, and that's when we need to try to come up with a compromise.

Franklin's idea to create an "agreement plan" is a good start. If you have a conflict with your parents, you might want to write out what it is that you want or would like to do and work together with your parents so that each point on your plan works for all of you.

QUICKIE

Gotta love a **quiz**! This issue's **Quickie** has 10 "friend-centric" Qs from our good friend **QuizMaster Anthony P.** See if you know the answers. Then go to **jonandjayne.com** to see if you're right. Click on "**QUICKIES.**" The password is **FRIENDS.** Catch the "Fresh Factoids" that pop up w/ each answer.

#1 What show's episode titles all began with the words "The One With . . ." or "The One Where . . ."?

#2 How old were Romeo and Juliet supposed to be?

#3 Speaking of Shakespeare, which of his plays inspired the 1999 movie *10 Things I Hate About You?*

#4 What famous song by '70s rock group Queen was featured at the end of the 2007 comedy *I Now Pronounce You Chuck and Larry*?

#5 To prove his love for one-time girlfriend Winona Ryder, Johnny "Captain Jack Sparrow" Depp got a tattoo. What did it say?

#6 How do you say the words "boyfriend" and "girlfriend" en Español?

#7 Which two characters sing "With a Little Help from My Friends" in the 2007 Beatles-inspired movie *Across the Universe*?

#8 What rapper sings the song "Best Friend"?

#9 What does the term "friends with benefits" mean?

#10 What's the name of SpongeBob SquarePants's best friend?

What a BLAST

In 1965, *(I Can't Get No) Satisfaction* by The Rolling Stones was on the top of the charts. A lot of our parents were just little kids back then. So, were our grandparents and their friends jammin' with The Stones?!

Got Satisfaction?

Making a **new** friend and/or finally **hooking** up with a new bf or gf can be really **satisfying**, especially when you've put so much **effort** into the whole process.

Even if you just start by **exchanging** a smile, you'll know that you've made an important first step in your **quest.** And every step that follows should be a little easier than the one before. If it hasn't happened yet for you, **don't stop** trying—keep making the effort. The end result will be **worth** it!

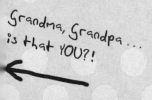

Grandma, Grandpa . . .
is that YOU?!

What's the one thing you would wanna tell the whole world if you could?

We asked . . . and you answered.
Here's what some of you had to say. ⟶

Get heard too. Go to jonandjayne.com and click on "Tell the World!" Then tell us what you have to say.

Look for your message to the world in an upcoming issue.

Tell the World

Hi!
Keff

Stop fighting!
Start peace!
Jaimie

We really should all work together and stop having enemies.
Samantha

Stop making nukes!
Taylor

Love people :)
Skylar

Don't worry so much.
Mike

Live in peace and love.
Ismael

Stop war, get peace, get over it!
Alina

Smarten up! If we work together, we wouldn't be having problems.
Trey

Get along & be peaceful.
Mallory

Stop the pain.
Carlla

Violence is not the answer.
Plinio

Hate is easy. Love takes courage!
Betania

Be Free!
Jeffrey

Stop global warming!
Charlee

Golf is not a sport.
Chris

Give money to the homeless.
Mohammad

Live your life minute to minute.
Antonella

Don't follow the crowd. Be yourself, because in the end it's not worth being like everyone else!!!
Kaitlyn

You shouldn't talk about people because it's immature.
Samantha

It's your life and your decisions. Do what you think is best for yourself and don't ever let anyone get in your way!
Kellina

Make right choices before you end up regretting what you did.
Jenn

No Internet?!

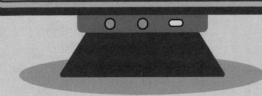

That's OK. You can still be part of our **7F community**. To get the answers to the Quickie and the Drama, simply send a postcard to our publisher's place:

HCI Teens
3201 SW 15th Street
Deerfield Beach, FL 33442
Attention: Quickie & Drama Answers

CYA!

Thanks for hanging w/ us!

We hope you had fun and got something out of our rantings and ramblings. Hope you liked the stories from our contributors. Got a story of your own? We'd really like to hear from you, so don't forget to visit us at **www.jonandjayne.com**. There's more to do & more to come. Join our 7F community and get heard!

~Jon & Jayne

A Little Help From Our Friends

Meet the #1 Crew

Hello, we're **Carol** and **Gary R.**, and we make it possible for "Jon and Jayne" to get their word out. We live in mostly sunny Florida with our two dogs, a cat, a parrot, and an iguana—and our son, Justin, who introduced us to Jon and Jayne.

My name is **Ashley K.** I am 15 years old. I'm currently in 9th grade. I plan on going to college for marine biology or writing.

Hey, I'm **Betania C.** I'm 15 years old. I was born and raised in Brazil until I was 8. Among ballet, playing soccer, and hanging out with my friends, I really enjoy writing. In fact, I plan on becoming a journalist in the future. My interest in writing began in elementary school when I used to write short stories as class work. From then on, I haven't been able to stop.

My name is **Billy M.** I'm 13. My hobbies are drawing, reading, remote control cars, video games, biking, and guitar. I'd like to make the world better for those who come after us and my small contribution to this right now is by participating in environmental clubs. I hope as I get older I can do more and really make a difference.

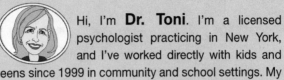

Hi, I'm **Dr. Toni**. I'm a licensed psychologist practicing in New York, and I've worked directly with kids and teens since 1999 in community and school settings. My specialty is running groups for preteen and teenage girls. I currently have a private practice in New York.

I'm **Candi G.** I'm 16. I was born in South Africa and moved to the U.S. when I was six. I play basketball and volleyball and run track for my school. I'm very outgoing. I've had a best friend named Jordan for about 6 years now. I'm a straight-A student, and some hobbies of mine are reading books, playing sports, boys, and shopping. I believe everything happens for a reason and we shouldn't waste any time of our lives with regrets or sadness. There are a thousand things going on without you if u miss your chance. <3

My name is **Crystal G.** I was born in Florida. I am currently finishing up my junior year of high school. In my spare time, I like to run, hang out with my friends, listen to music, and write, which has been my passion since I can remember.

My name's **Emily O.** I'm 15. I play basketball and run cross country and am trying track this year. I love playing sports. I have great friends, most of which I made in high school, and we hang out all the time. Our favorite things to do are go to the gym, Panera Bread, and hang out with all our other friends. I like school and do well. I take honors classes and get mostly As. I'm a really nice and caring person and the complete opposite of aggressive. I love meeting new people. =)

I'm **Eric D.** I'm 15. I like to skateboard and play PS2 Army games. I was born in California. My best friend's name is Vinnie—we've been friends since 4th grade. I don't like school very much, but I like to go to socialize. I like Bob Marley and rock music.

Hi, I'm **Franklin B.** I'm 16. I'm friends with a diverse group of people. The best part of hanging out with my friends is seeing movies together, but the massive amount of calling and texting is the worst. I like exploring new places and meeting new people during vacation. It's my belief that family should always come first.

I'm **Jen F.** and I'm 16. I was born on Long Island, NY. I play basketball for my school and run track and cross-country. I like to hang out with my friends and do different things. My best friends are Alex, Chett, and Beth, and we call each other the rectangle. I get along with mostly everyone, but I'm known to have a really big attitude.

Hi, I'm **Joseph C.** I'm 16. I'm on the football, wrestling, and track teams at my high school. When I'm hanging out with my friends, I like being places where there are lots of different kinds of people. I really think that doing good in school will take you a long way in life.

Hi, I'm **Kaitlyn R.** I'm 15. I loooove shopping, hanging out with my friends, and listening to music. I hate doing nothing. I think global warming is scary and that something has to be done about it. The things about school I dislike the most are homework and tests! They're so annoying.

Hi, my name's **Kellina M.** I'm a freshman in high school. The sport that I enjoy most is basketball. I've been playing organized basketball since I was seven years old. I like to listen to hip hop and rap music a lot. When I finally graduate, I want to go to Notre Dame University. I have an 11-year-old brother and a 13-year-old sister. I have many friends, but I have the greatest people as my best friends.

Hi, my name is **Lexi S.** I'm in 8th grade. I have two dogs named Holly and Maggie. My hobbies are playing soccer, playing lacrosse, hanging out with my friends, skiing, and swimming. When I get older, I hope to be a professional soccer player or a doctor. My overall goal in life is to be successful.

Hi! My name is **Samantha D.** and I am 12 years old. I live with my parents, brother, and our dog Bella. They're all very supportive of me. I was the starting goalie of the school soccer team and I play travel soccer. My favorite food is filet mignon, and I love sports! My two favorite sports are soccer and karate. I also love dogs. I don't like scary movies, marshmallows, or mean people.

My name is **Skylar H.** I am 15. I have been doing karate since the age of three and I'm a junior black belt. I play on the JV basketball team at my school. My friends are very important to me and so is my family. I like to talk online to my friends and on the phone. I love watching teen drama movies about relationships, and I like reading books about drama also. I really enjoy working with kids and people.

This is **QuizMaster Anthony P**. I love movies and music and books and art and TV (especially Ernie Kovacs—look him up online!). I have worked in book publishing my entire career, including three years in children's books. I'm a happy stepdad to twins, which keeps life interesting.

My name is **Taylor W**. I'm 14 years old and I'm a freshman in high school. I'm part of the BSS. I listen to heavy metal and nothing else but that. My hobbies are playing my guitar, riding my dirt bike, and riding my bicycle around town with my friends.

The Grammar Expert

In this book, Jon, Jayne, and their friends take lots of shortcuts and liberties with the written word. It's fun, easy, and sometimes quicker to write or text that way.

In formal writing, those shortcuts, slang spellings, and inconsistencies should be avoided **AT ALL COSTS**, and every sentence should end with some sort of punctuation. !?;):

Fortunately for Jon and Jayne, this ~~ain't~~ isn't a formal piece of writing meant to be emulated like great poetry. You'll find no iambic pentameter here.*

—Carol

*But you might find it on the website. Search for the hidden rollover.

Where Can I Find . . . ?

A
acquaintances versus friends, 67–68
"All Roads Lead to Rome," 55–57
Ashley's story, 65–66

B
B3C stance, 79
"Battle of the Cliques, The," 61–64
Betania's story, 61–64
Billy's story, 22–24
"Black Sheep Squadron, The," 58–59
body language, 15, 31–34
body-language chart, 33–34
bullies and gangs, 59–60

C
challenges, 43
chances, taking, 38, 42
charisma, 41–43, 44
cliques, 53–54
"Clumsy Me," 19
confidence, 41–43, 44
conflict with parents. *see* vent.
conundrums and solutions, 84–94
conversations, 35–39
courage, 41–43, 44
creative visualization, 29–30
crew member bios, 113–117
Crystal's story, 98–100

D
dead-end questions, 35, 39
drama, the, 10–11

E
Eric's story, 45–47

F
first impressions, 13–15
Franklin's story, 101–103
friends, versus acquaintances, 67–68

G
gangs. *see* bullies and gangs.
gossip, 75. *see also* rumors.
"Got a Pen?" 49–51

H
"He Said, She Said," 73

I
(I Can't Get No) Satisfaction, 106
imagination, using. *see* creative visualization.

impressing a girl (Jon's advice), 25
impressing a guy (Jayne's advice), 25
impressions. *see* first impressions.
insecurities, 31
interests, 36

J

Joseph's story, 55–57
"Judging a Book by Its Cover," 16–18
Kait's story, 49–51
kenpo, 60

L

Lexi's story, 16–18
love broker, being a, 69–72

M

"My Agreement Plan," 101–103

N

"Not for Me," 65–66

O

open-ended questions, 35, 37, 39
outsiders, 64

P

parents, conflict with. *see* vent.
problems. *see* conundrums and solutions.
"Putting Yourself Out There," 45–47

Q

questions. *see* open-ended questions; dead-end questions.
quickie ,104–105
quirks, 14

R

respect, 42
Rolling Stones, 106
rumors, 75–79

S

Samantha's story, 81–83
scenarios, 7–9
school clubs, 57
secrets, sharing, 68
self-esteem, 41–42, 44
Shari's story, 19–21
"Sneaking Around," 98–100
survey, 40
"Sydney, Soccer, and Me," 81–83

T

Taylor's story, 58–59
Tell the world, 108–109

V

vent, 95–97
violence prevention, 60
violence, school. *see* bullies and gangs.
visualization, creative. *see* creative visualization.

W

"Weird Kid in Art Class, The," 22–24

C U SOON!

Jayne ♡'s Jon

Who WROTE That?!

THE END . . .

. . . Not

You're Invited...

Check out Jon & Jayne's Guide to Throwing, Going to, and "Surviving" Parties and other issues at www.jonandjayne.com

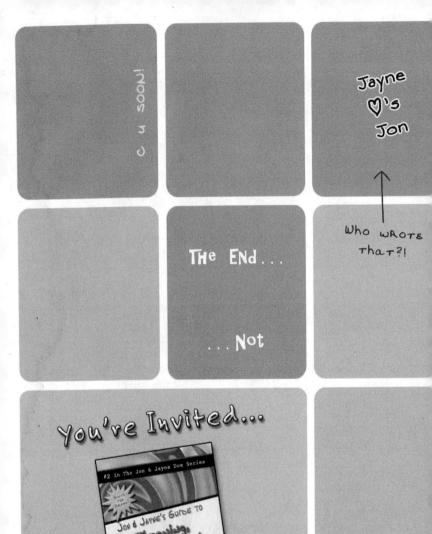

There's a lot more to come